MARTHA'S VINEYARD
THROUGH TIME
The Present in the Past

A. C. THEOKAS

AMERICA
THROUGH TIME®
ADDING COLOR TO AMERICAN HISTORY

America Through Time is an imprint of Fonthill Media LLC
www.through-time.com
office@through-time.com

Published by Arcadia Publishing by arrangement with Fonthill Media LLC
For all general information, please contact Arcadia Publishing:
Telephone: 843-853-2070
Fax: 843-853-0044
E-mail: sales@arcadiapublishing.com
For customer service and orders:
Toll-Free 1-888-313-2665

www.arcadiapublishing.com

First published 2019

Copyright © A. C. Theokas 2019

ISBN 978-1-63500-101-3

Typeset in Mrs Eaves XL Serif Narrow
Printed and bound in England

These two photographs show something of the exceptionality of Martha's Vineyard. Pointed arch windows, a characteristic of the Carpenter Gothic style, are shown in the top image. Examples of this type of architecture can certainly be seen on the mainland, but its proliferation and grouping here has shaped this island's unique mood and feel. The dawn of a new winter's day is seen from Ocean Park in the bottom photo. This park remains an important design element of the only town in the entire United States to be specifically planned for tourism. [*author*]

The changes to this island's physical environment are certainly matched by those in the people themselves. How they relate to the camera is but one example. The top photo (detail page 17) shows the stiff and unsmiling pose typical of the period, likely due to required long exposure times and Victorian culture. The bottom photo, taken in Vineyard Haven (C. 1935, *mvm*) illustrates how camera technology allowed a candid shot to include the smiling woman at right. The fountain still exists, but is now a planter next to the 'stone building' at the other end of Main Street.

Island communities are the original alternative societies. That is why so many mainlanders envy them. Of their nature they break down the multiple alienations of industrial and suburban man. Some vision of Utopian belonging, of social blessedness, of an independence based on cooperation, haunts them all.

John Fowles, *Islands*

INTRODUCTION

Photographs of Martha's Vineyard abound in galleries, calendars, magazines and hefty hardcovers. In contrast to these color-saturated images are "vintage" black and whites easily found on the Internet. These images not only connote aspects of island life, but also something of the medium itself as an analytic art form capable of capturing that "decisive moment." The resulting photographs might be part of a themed compilation or individually displayed.

This small volume is not intended to add to any of this. The focus here is not photographs as such, but the passage of time. Paired images taken from the same vantage point, but separated by decades, are on the pages that follow. The change shown can be slight or significant and, if the latter, does not necessarily mean progress. This format brings changes to the island's social, environmental and commercial landscape into a tighter focus. They record "modernization" moving at varying rates through different periods across this island and might be of interest to anyone concerned about its future development.

Shown here are more than changes in architectural form, patterns of commerce or how we relate to the land and to the sea. It is also an expression of photography as a nostalgic art evoking a twilight sentiment. The camera may put an end to time, but photos are a perpetual reminder of its passing. A nineteenth-century sepia of people posing on a cottage porch is more than merely "quaint." We cannot completely sidestep the thought that while the cottage may have survived, they have not. As Sontag put it, "to take a photograph is to participate in another person's (or thing's) mortality, vulnerability, mutability. Precisely by slicing out this moment and freezing it, all photographs testify to time's relentless melt."

Martha's Vineyard was unveiled, quite literally, at a glacial pace during the close of the last episode of continent-wide geologic activity. Twenty thousand years ago the great North American ice sheet, over a mile thick in places, receded, its overbearing tonnage scouring and sculpting the land beneath it. Island terrain still exhibits evidence of that slow yet dynamic process, moraines and outwash plains. The location of Martha's

Vineyard and nearby Nantucket are not coincidental. The shapes of the moraines indicate that the ice did not originally flow as a continuous single sheet but in lobes. When it retreated, the debris originally pushed forward by the advancing ice was more elevated where lobes had merged to form "high spots" that would remain exposed as the ice retreated. Meltwater later caused the sea to rise until that last link to the mainland was permanently awash, making Martha's Vineyard an island. It is composed of, in contrast to the hard bedrock coastline of northern New England, malleable glacial deposits of sand and clay that are no match for that self-same sea that yet continues, in fits and starts, to shape a coastline in slow retreat.

By the seventeenth century, the island had become the established home of the Wampanoags or "People of the First Light," easterners who also occupied the area east of Narraganset Bay from Rhode Island to Cape Cod and Nantucket. The Wampanoag referred to the island as *No-Pe* or "land amongst the waters," or *Capawok*, "place of refuge." The first European to chart the island was Bartholomew Gosnold, in 1602. While sometimes credited with naming it both after his daughter and its supposed "vineyards," this is unlikely; lands were not named after commoners at that time. Moreover, early deeds, wills, and other official documents indicate it was also once referred to as *Martin's* Vineyard. Exactly how the current name came to predominate is not exactly known. It may well be that both are corruptions of some Indian word and not English at all. Today, however, it is simply and affectionately referred to as "the Vineyard."

Vineyarders speak of up-Island and down-Island. Up-Island is the western area, comprised of the three towns of Aquinnah, Chilmark and West Tisbury. Down-Island includes the eastern towns of Tisbury, Oak Bluffs and Edgartown. The sailing term "heading up" means to turn into the wind, but it can also mean to increase your longitude by heading west or decrease it by heading east. And so, we have up-Island and down-Island. It is significant that, despite their island location and proximity, the three down-Island towns acquired and preserved distinctive architectural styles. They have not undergone the sustained commercial downturns or spasms of ill-conceived modernity, as have so many mainland towns. In contrast to the relative stability of the island's townscapes, its old agricultural landscape has undergone more substantial change.

DOWN-ISLAND

The easternmost town, Edgartown, was the first. Thomas Mayhew, a Watertown native, purchased Martha's Vineyard for forty pounds from two English noblemen with conflicting titles to it, a bargain even at that time. His son, Thomas Jr., was appointed as its first governor by the governor of New York, Thomas Lovelace, in 1670. The young Mayhew was also made Lord of the Manor of Tisbury since early colonial America had exported the customs and social structure of feudal England. To propitiate his own superior, the Duke of York, Lovelace suggested that the name of this early settlement be changed from Great Harbour to Edgar Towne, in honor of the Duke's young son.

Unfortunately, his son had died, but the news had not yet crossed the Atlantic. The name, however, remained, leaving Edgartown the only town so named anywhere.

The first street was Main Street, laid out perpendicular to the harbor. Other significant streets in its physical development were North and South Water Streets that form a continuous road bisected by Main Street and runs along most of the harbor frontage and North and South Pease's Point Way to the east. The town proper is laid out like a grid that slightly curves to follow the shoreline of the harbor which it abuts. Except for a small area that extends out along Main Street, the town is basically bounded by North and South Water Streets and Pease's Point Way.

It would be incorrect to assume that little survives of Edgartown's period as a major port for the whaling industry that prospered from 1835 to its decline after the Civil War. Edgartown's residential architecture constructed during this period is evidence enough. Until about 1860, the only source of oil was whale oil produced through a very lucrative, if dangerous and brutal, business. A young man might make a decent living sheep farming or fishing, but whaling could make you truly wealthy. Those that managed to do so have left a legacy of Federalist style and Greek Revival homes that give Edgartown its character today.

The Federalist style is typified by fan shaped windows over the front door, delicate ornaments of garlands and urns, balustrades, and Palladian windows on the second floor above the main entrance, all providing a delicate decorative counterpoint to the typically rectangular or square front façade. The Greek Revival style is by far the dominant architectural style in Edgartown. Its popularity was due to the concurrence of a period of whaling prosperity and the strong attraction to the newly appreciated forms of classical Greece. Greek Revival residences were usually painted white to resemble the white marble of impressive and costly public buildings. Simple moldings, heavy cornices, gables with pediments, unadorned friezes and low roof slopes are typical features. Later trends in architectural style tended not to cross the Vineyard Sound. Federalist and Greek Revival styles remained in favor longer than on the mainland and outnumber later arrivals such as the Queen Anne or Shingle Style, styles just as scarce in the town ten miles to the west.

The earliest English name for Oak Bluffs was the "Easternmost chop of Homes Hole" and is ascribed to Thomas Mayhew. The plural, "chops," signifies the entrance to a channel and so today we have East Chop and West Chop. The boundaries of Oak Bluffs were set in 1880 when it was incorporated with the name Cottage City. Prior to that, Oak Bluffs was mostly composed of the Daggett farm extending from the coast on either side of Farm Pond roughly to County Road. Oak Bluffs did not begin with incremental additions by other colonists, but rather through its initial establishment as a religious center on the shores of Squash Meadow Pond (now Sunset Lake). The first "camp meeting" was held in the summer of 1834.

Oak Bluffs has beginnings unique not only to the island, but the country at large. It first started as an adaptation of the religious camp meeting phenomenon popular in nineteenth-century America. Open-air revivals that proliferated throughout the South, Midwest, and eventually the Northeast, offered the chance to reject one's depravities. Reform and piety awaited the penitent sinner. The second stage of growth was the commercial expansion designed to attract and host summer visitors, thus making it the only town in America entirely planned and laid out specifically for tourism. The architecture of these two extraordinary communities, the one offering spiritual rebirth and the other saltwater taffy, combined to create, as Weiss puts it, "a peculiar place, a magical environment, a work of art."

Martha's Vineyard was fertile ground for the establishment and growth of its own Methodist camp meeting community. The initial site was established with the form typical of camp-meeting grounds: a circular arrangement of tents around seating for the congregants and a preacher's pulpit at the center. Known initially as Wesleyan Grove, its annual growth was due not only to its growing reputation as pastoral Eden-like location, but also because it was on an island whose isolation offered a sense of otherworldliness, a place free from the distractions and disturbances suffered by sister mainland groups. It also assuaged anxiety for men at sea as whalers and countered overwrought introspection brought about by the island's isolation. The number of tents grew until what became a large camp was ultimately transformed by the more orderly development of discrete neighborhood units, town planning on a small scale.

This Methodist Camp Ground became, due to the tranquil beauty of its island setting, more than a short-term annual event. Members stayed longer and, one by one, tents were replaced by permanent wooden structures. The huge demand for canvas brought about by the Civil War may also have contributed to this conversion. Each cottage was anything but plain with its rich detail and color. Island lore has it that this was to compensate for the constraints of the small footprint once occupied by a tent. Large tents were replaced by small cottages. These details merged into a consistent Gothic vernacular applied by anonymous carpenters. Each cottage had its own articulation, but it also contributed to a shared motif of geometry, proportion and size throughout, resulting in the Camp Ground-wide character and symbolic richness that is still admired today. The cottages possess an eccentricity and edginess resulting from incongruities of scale. They are small yet avoid the appearance of a miniature house where every element is shrunk to the same proportions. The wide double-door entrance and enlarged second-story openings are out of scale with the rest of the structure, a deliberate design feature rarely seen elsewhere.

The focal area of the grounds where members gathered to hear the preacher's exhortation was also in need of a more permanent structure. The present iron tabernacle was constructed in 1879 by the Springfield Mass. engineering firm of Dwight and Hoyt, but the actual designer(s) remain anonymous. The three-tiered signature roof is supported by slender iron columns, giving it the overall appearance of floating in space. It is only slightly larger than the old canvas tabernacle it replaced with the current stage occupying the same location and orientation of the original preacher's platform. It may be difficult to classify as a specific design style, but both it and the encircling cottages remain as the high-water mark of a cultural tide long since receded.

Why Gothic stylistic elements? Unlike the streetscapes in Edgartown lined with Greek Revival facades, Oak Bluffs builders were instead guided by the ecclesiastical idiom of Medieval Europe. Contemporary accounts of this Methodist community suggest there was, in the minds of its builders, some sense that the design of the Gothic cathedrals of Europe were more expressive of their own revelatory ecstasies than was the coolness of the Classical line and dispassionate Protestantism. The camp meeting movement, like other utopian societies so prevalent in nineteenth-century America, has long since vanished. The Wesleyan Grove may no longer perform as the psychic core of Oak Bluffs, but it continues as the contemplative setting originally envisioned.

The Wesleyan Grove may have occupied a peaceful location, but entrepreneurs among the membership knew that privies, crude beds and community cooking would not attract the wealthier secular visitor. The attraction of the oak grove left its impression on all those who visited and as their number increased the potential of the island as a summer destination along fewer religious lines was realized. To attract the less pious to their seaside idyll, more comforts and a commercial core were needed. One of them, Foxborough native Erastus Carpenter and straw-hat magnate, decided he would not only build his own cottage outside the campgrounds, he would also bring in investors to build hundreds of others. The Land and Wharf Company was formed, and Robert Morris Copeland, a landscape architect, was hired to design the new community. An ad ran in the *Vineyard Gazette* for "cheap and quiet homes by the seashore ...plans available for beautiful cottages from $300 to $1000." This was the beginning of Cottage City. Carpenter had the foresight to realize Copeland's initial design presentation was too dense, and despite the likely loss in profit, ordered that more open space be added. This resulted in the creation of Ocean Park and Waban Park, as well as over ten smaller parks. Ocean Park especially set the tone for arriving visitors by performing two key functions. First, arriving steamship passengers were welcomed by its receptive form. It was the first view disembarking passengers had of Cottage City. Secondly, it was bounded not by cottages, but by grand summer homes that were far from cottages. Visitors arrived at a place of tranquil eloquence. It had become a destination.

Cottage City lasted until 1907 when Oak Bluffs was adopted as something more synonymous with its origins. An early plan by Copeland shows over sixty parcels on Circuit Avenue that were meant for residential development. It soon became clear, however, that the few grocery stores, lodging houses and other sundry merchants confined to the Camp Ground could not meet all the needs of a growing summer population, and by the end of the century, this plan had been reconsidered. Circuit Avenue acquired four-story hotels, fancy goods shops, and hardware stores with the Island House, The Wigwam and the Pawnee House among the more well-known. Early post cards of a crowd-filled affluent Circuit Ave are evocative of a Golden Age.

Prior to the conversion of tents to cottages, the close of day brought a change in atmosphere. Hundreds of kerosene lamps combined to create a cumulative glow from within the white canvas tents, adding to the mood of a pastoral paradise, an effect lost when cottages replaced them. Perhaps it was this that gave Carpenter the idea to create the "Illumination." It began as a marketing strategy to, at the height of the summer season, garland the cottages that bordered Owens Park with paper oriental lanterns. This tradition was eventually moved into the grove, but likely for a more communal than lighthearted sentiment. It is a tradition that survives to this day.

Vineyard Haven may look the youngest of the three major towns on the island, but it is an old town. By the 1880s, it was the island's major port and had a larger number of businesses than either of the other towns. Its original name, Holmes Hole, is the oldest place name on the island. The term "hole" refers to a small inlet of water affording shelter to boats, e.g. Woods Hole. A vote was held to change the name and "Vineyard Haven" was adopted in 1871 when it was well over 225 years old. Apparently, the use of "hole" did not appeal to a citizenry whose town was every bit as prosperous and picturesque as its two sister towns. Unfortunately, this rebirth was short-lived when the town was all but destroyed by fire twelve years later. Over sixty buildings were destroyed as well as the numerous elms that graced and shaded Main Street. A smaller portion of Vineyard Haven's early appearance can be seen along William St. running parallel to Main St., and where the fire did not quite reach, but the original scenic streetscape, the town's legacy to the island, was lost forever.

William Street was the second street laid out in Holmes Hole in 1831. Most of the properties there, built between 1830 and 1860, are of the Greek Revival style. Sizes vary from moderately small to imposing and were the work of early Holmes Hole builders without benefit of known architects, much as the builders of the Oak Bluffs Camp Ground cottages. Today it is a historic district and represents the single best-preserved area of mid-nineteenth century architecture in Vineyard Haven.

Up-Island

Heading west from Vineyard Haven along State Road takes you up-Island. Commercial development thins, and there are moments in the landscape that suggest little has changed since the nineteenth century. Each island town had its specialty; whaling in Edgartown, Tisbury had shipping and piloting, Chilmark's was (and still is) fishing, but West Tisbury's was farming, and it is where most of the remaining island farms are now located, although not as self-sufficient as their predecessors. Eventually, you come to Old Mill Pond and, just pass that, Alley's General Store, both markers of island history. This is West Tisbury village and like Edgartown, many of its grand homes were built with profits from whaling. A former academy, library, agricultural hall and Congregational church all survive, allowing it to look much as it did 150 years ago.

The up-Island landscape of the late-nineteenth century was as variegated as it is today, although not in quite the same way. One clue to this is found in the classic New England stonewalls found winding through wooded areas or along roadsides lined with heavy growth. Why would anyone labor to build stone walls in wooded areas? The answer is they would not. When these walls were built, there was no woodland. In fact, there were few, if any, trees there at all. The stone walls are the result of neatly piled rocks gathered during the farm clearing of the eighteenth century. Early island agriculture combined with sheep and dairy farms kept pastures and fields clear except for the occasional marker tree. The fuel required for later brickworks also served to reduce woodland coverage.

The decline of agriculture and sheep farming resulted in reclamation by second-growth forest. The first summer after the land is released back into the wild, formerly plowed fields are overcome with weeds, after five years briar, birch and juniper sprout from seeds brought in by birds. Within forty years, new secondary growth fills in the landscape, making it appear it had never been cultivated, but it is not virgin forest. This process of farm abandonment combined with forest reclamation may seem, in the current climate, as a victory for conservation. At the time, however, it was a sign of failure and abandonment.

Boulders can allude to the past not only through their arrangement in walls, but as single standing stones. Each can provide some clue about the culture that has come before, something beyond serving as simple focal point to anchor a landscape. The Cromlech of Quitsa recalls Neolithic structures found in Europe. This cromlech or dolmen suggests that Vikings were once here. Sugarloaf Rock, a legendary Indian site, was later used as a deed marker. Toad Rock was purportedly an Indian post office, the eye enlarged to contain message tokens. Lovers Rock, a massive glacial erratic at the other end of the island on the beach at Oak Bluffs, was a site popular for young bathers in the late nineteenth century. It is still there, somewhere, but long since reclaimed by the sea.

"Charming" or "quaint" have been used to describe Menemsha, the tiny fishing community located at the end of North Road. True enough, but it is still a place of tough work. Moreover, it is unlikely that fishermen can today afford the cottages there as they once did. Menemsha (one supposed meaning is "still water") is part a of Chilmark initially known as Creekville and named after the narrow waterway leading from Vineyard Sound into Menemsha Pond. The creek was dredged and widened in 1905, allowing for more berths and a wider channel to the sea. Unfortunately, Menemsha, like Vineyard Haven, suffered a major disaster. Despite the appearance of the shingled shanties, lobster shacks and weathered dock, it is the newest community, in terms of its construction, on the island. The Great Hurricane of 1938 swept it away at a time when hurricanes were little understood or predicted. It has long since recovered and is the home of the island's fishing fleet and a popular fish market.

Beetlebung Corner punctuates an up-Island journey to Gay Head. This is the center of the Town of Chilmark. To the right as you enter the "corner" is the Town Hall. And to the left is the town's commercial center, that once consisted of a blacksmith and Mayhew's general store. Beetlebung refers to a species of the Tupelo tree, *Nyssa sylvatica*. The adopted term likely derives from the local use of the hardwood from these trees once used to make mallets or "beetles" used to tap "bungs" into the bunghole of barrels and casks.

Further up island from Chilmark is the town of Aquinnah, formerly known as Gay Head. This was the original home of the island's first inhabitants, the Wampanoag, the site of the historic and colorful clay cliffs, and the location of the island's last operational lighthouse. Although it is now also the site of many large summer homes, the year-round population is small, less than 350 at the 2010 census. The clay cliffs at Gay Head, now a national landmark, were exposed by glacial activity and not the result of it. The pigmented clay has lost some of its vibrancy due to erosion, but it is nonetheless still indicative of the huge river delta that once flowed into the Atlantic from the interior and laid down successive layers of different material over time that were the result of the stressed ecosystem of the late Mesozoic. The glacier's much later southward motion pushed immense quantities of rock, sand and clay ahead of itself, creating ripples in the landscape, bringing this record of a challenged climate to the surface. While the action of the last glacier occurred some 20,000 years ago, that of the cliffs at Gay Head speak of a landscape well over 4,000 times older. It was, until recently an abused landscape, the colorful clays mined for an ingredient for paint and, much later, when New Agers swathed themselves in mud from the cliffs. The cliffs are now protected, not only from mud pie players, but also fossil hunters.

Atop the cliffs at the Gay Head is the lighthouse built in 1849 on a site critical to marine navigation. Recently, it was newsworthy in that it was physically moved from its original location because of the erosion that brought the cliff side to within forty feet. Before the age of electricity, lighthouses wrestled with the best way to project a warning beam to all nearby mariners. Shortly after its construction, the Great Exhibition was held in London. One of the exhibits was the Fresnel lens designed by Augustin Jean Fresnel. Its design used stacked prisms to permit the construction of lenses of a large aperture and short focal length without the weight and volume required by a lens of conventional design. After the London exhibition, the lens was purchased by the government for 16,000 dollars or about 500,000 in today's money. The first such lens used in the United States, it is now on display at the Martha's Vineyard Museum.

Although the island's bygone industries consisted mainly of seagoing enterprises such as whaling, fisheries, commercial shipping and the like, it was also home to several inland manufactories such as salt works, paint factories, brickworks, grist mills, tanneries, and carding and weaving mills. Unlike the mainland, however, these were not concentrated in the towns nor were they year-round enterprises. They tended to be sited up-Island where necessary waterpower was available to drive grinding wheels or carding and fulling hammers. These early industries never really provided steady employment and gradually lost to competition from the mainland. Evidence of their existence remains in only a few places such as the site of the Satinet Mill in West Tisbury or a bladeless windmill that can be seen from North Road in Chilmark.

By the end of the nineteenth century, however, the island economy increasingly relied on something never envisioned at its beginning: tourism. Martha's Vineyard had become a destination for a new middle class who sought more than simple escape from urban cacophony and sunbaked manure. They came to consume the exotic and return with a trinket or two. Arriving by the thousands, they carried a new awareness of the pleasures and intrigue of the boundary between the land and sea. True, this occurred elsewhere, but Martha's Vineyard had that added allure only an island can provide. A following companion book, *Martha's Vineyard Through Time: Tourism and the Cleansing Sea* looks at the changes this brought. Here, however, the focus is on the iconic architecture and landscape that summer visitors still come to enjoy.

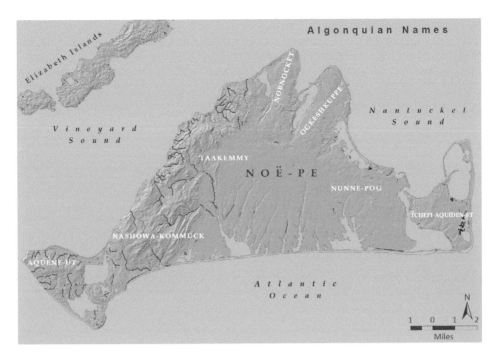

MAPS OLD AND NEW: The top map, labeled with Wampanoag place names, shows the island before white settlers arrived. East to west these are Tchepi-audient-et or "end of the island place," Nunne-pog or "fresh pond or water place," Ogkseshkuppe or "the damp thicket or woods," Nobnocket or "at the place of dry land," Taakemmy or "where he or she strikes it," Nashowa Kommuck or "the half-way house" and Aqeune-it, or "land under the hill." Eventually, by degree and decree, these were replaced by their present-day Anglicized town names. Town boundaries are in yellow and the island's major roads in black in the map at bottom. [mvc]

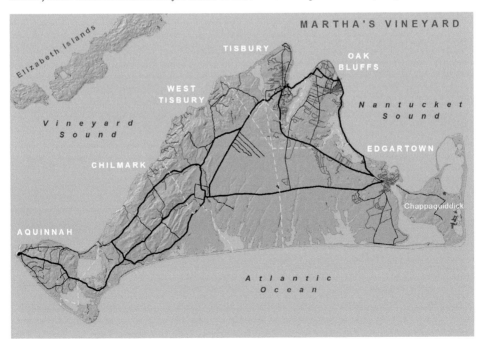

CHAPPAQUIDDICK FERRY: At a little over 500 feet from Edgartown, Chappaquiddick has both a sense of proximity and remoteness. The first automobile was ferried over in 1912, but scheduled service did not begin until over twenty years later with the creation of the first ever self-propelled barge made by island boat builders. The name on the top image, *On Time*, does not refer to a timetable, but to the fact that the first boat was built on time in the space of nine days in Edgartown. Plans to expand the service over the years were considered, but in the end, this ferry has run in much the same way as it has since 1935, when first established. C. 1955 [mvm]

OLD SCULPIN GALLERY: This was once the site of Dr. Daniel Fisher's (see page 27) whale-oil refinery, although this building was not part of it. Its original usage was as a mill for grinding grain, flour storage and a sail loft. In the 1920s, it was converted to a marine-carpenter shop by the memorable and beloved Manual Swartz Roberts, premier builder of catboats, the basic workboat of the island. One of the oldest buildings on the island, it remains a home for the creative spirit as an art gallery and educational space using Swartz' nickname, "Old Sculpin." L. Convery 1986 [*macris*]

DOCK STREET: Once owned by the entrepreneurial Dr. Fisher, this area is now public property. Years ago, it was called Steamboat Wharf when it was a stop for steamers from Woods Hole and New Bedford. The Chappaquiddick ferry, at the end of the dock, still runs from here. The workshops that once lined Dock Street, such as the bilge pump shop and hardtack bakery have been replaced by souvenir shops and ice cream outlets. C. 1960 [*mvm*]

THE OLD DOCK: The flotsam along the dock is symbolic of the decline of Edgartown's once thriving whaling industry. The cannon is from a former whaling ship, the *Mary*, while at the center of the image is a try pot, once used to render and remove the oil from whale blubber, perhaps from the same vessel. The modern view shows how little remains of the configuration of the early dock. The try pot, however, survives as a flowerpot in the garden next to the Old Sculpin Gallery (see back cover). Baldwin Coolidge. C. 1880 [*nhs*]

EDGARTOWN YACHT CLUB: This is the bottom of Main Street, with Dock Street on the right. An early version of the yacht club is shown with private businesses across the street that did not yet cater to tourists. But the yacht club, founded in 1905, presaged changes to come as it represented the shift in boating from commercial to recreational. The Old Whaling Church can be seen in the distance, top photo, but trees have altered that long view here as they have done elsewhere. C. 1890 [*mvm*]

MAIN AND WATER STREETS: Edgartown was once a port of entry for whalers and other vessels and their cargoes had to be passed through customs. The Customs House was above the clothing store in the Greek Revival structure at right. Records suggest it was built before 1828, just as the whaling industry was reaching its peak. The top photo also shows the open appearance Main Street once had. The spire of the Old Whaling Church can be seen in the distant center. C. 1890 [*mvm*]

EDGARTOWN NATIONAL BANK: Built in 1855 on the intersection known as the Four Corners, it began as the Martha's Vineyard National Bank. It was the first brick building in Edgartown and remains one of only three. It is important historically as prior to this all banking was done off-island. It remains a bank building and has undergone little external alteration after over 160 years. The streetlamp on the sidewalk in this early photo ran on kerosene, once a reviled word here as it signaled the end of the whaling industry. C. 1875 [mvm]

EDGARTOWN GOTHIC: This early street scene shows a rare example of a building in Edgartown with elements of Gothic architecture, a style more closely associated with Oak Bluffs. It was originally known as "Gothic Hall" for its second-storey windows and was doubtless a showpiece when it was built in the 1830s. With little alteration over the years, except for the small addition at right, it has cycled through various businesses; meat market, ice-cream parlor and, perhaps, "Eddy's Refrigerators." C. 1890 [*mvm*]

MAIN STREET: The top image shows an unobstructed view along Main St in Edgartown looking east towards the harbor. Due to the island's separation from the mainland, local architecture tended to be conservative and idiosyncratic. The early architecture along Edgartown's Main St is a perfect example of this with its collection of Greek Revival, "modern," Gothic and Colonial styles. A sign for the post office can just be seen at right. The bottom image indicates that only the Gothic building remains. C. 1890. [*mvm*]

THE VINEYARD GAZETTE: Site of the old *Gazette* office at the corner of North Water St and Main Street. At the left is what was the old Customs House and the grand Federalist homes are ahead on North Water St. Notice the "Market" signboard here and in the following photo, indicating the ground floor market. The structure that has replaced it is angled to address the intersection, an urban design device used elsewhere, such as Oxford Circus in London. C. 1900 [*mvm*]

MAIN ST EAST: The building to the right of center, influenced by Greek Revival proportions, is the only one that remains. Despite this, the overall appearance of the bottom end of Main St in Edgartown is preserved. The commercial character of the street, however, has changed with the times. It is not likely that coal is now sold here, or anywhere else, on Main Street. C. 1890 [*mvm*]

MAIN STREET FOOTRACE: Shown is a well-attended footrace on Main Street in Edgartown, a 100-yard dash won by Marcus Jernegan, who later taught history at The University of Chicago. The edge of the brick bank building can just be discerned left of center in the distance. Note the sign "R.G. Shute" known for his photography of the island. The Shutes, father and son, were famous for their stereoscopic photographs, a collection of which is now kept in the Boston Public Library. C. 1893 [mvm]

THE METHODIST CHURCH: Now referred to as the Old Whaling Church, it was completed in 1849. The tower clock was installed twenty years later. The classical Greek and Roman elements (pediment and columns) were likely influenced by earlier generations of British architects, particularly Christopher Wren, who designed many of London's churches after the Great Fire of 1666. This influence of Georgian architecture is little seen elsewhere on the island and was a style shunned by the Camp Ground Methodists in Oak Bluffs. C. 1900 [mvm]

THE FISHER HOUSE: The Dr. Daniel Fisher home at the beginning of Main St belonged to early Edgartown's premier businessman, who supplied the whaling industry with hardtack, established a bank and owned a whale oil refinery and spermaceti candle manufactory. It is a classic example of the Federalist style influenced by the symmetry of earlier Georgian architecture. It has lasted in part because of its unusual construction; it was framed with pine soaked in lime for two years and only copper or brass nails were used. No longer a private residence, today it is used for functions and conferences. C. 1890 [*mvm*]

NORTH WATER STREET: The houses on the left side of North Water Street heading away from Main Street (on the right in this view) are slightly cambered and not parallel to the street. They were sited this way to allow for the best view of vessels as they rounded Cape Pogue and entered Edgartown Harbor. There were, at that the time of their construction, few homes or trees on the north side of the street to block that view. Shown here is a prime example of the Federalist architecture there, the Jared Fisher house with its boxlike roof, attenuated detail and muted pilasters. The Rotograph Company. C. 1900

"ACADEMY STREET": Quality education was important in Edgartown in the early nineteenth century for the children of a prosperous whaling community. This street was once so regarded because of two academies: the Davis Academy shown at left (fronting Davis Lane) and Thaxter Academy (not in view). The Davis Academy, built in 1836, was a purpose-built building and is today a private residence. These photos show how little Edgartown's neighborhoods have changed in appearance and are worth a wander. C. 1880 [*mvm*]

CIRCUIT AVENUE: The building at left remains, but little else. Designed in the popular mock-Asian style, it began as Macy's and is today a restaurant mainstay. The Civil War memorial still exists, but has been moved. The vertical sign of the Wigwam can be seen at center. There are no sidewalks as the avenue was intended for promenading, not motor traffic. Today, cars, little leaf Lindens and change in architecture have altered this prospect of Oak Bluffs' high street. C. 1895 [*Valentine and Sons*]

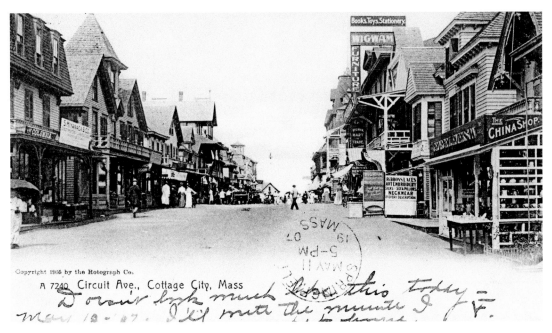

A 7240 Circuit Ave., Cottage City, Mass

EARLY POSTCARD: "Doesn't look much like this today" wrote the sender at the bottom of this postcard, referring to the image made only two years earlier. The tower of the Wigwam Block rises above the others on the easterly side with its elongated vertical sign. This was the headquarters for "sea shore supplies" that included not only water wings and toy boats, but also crockery, draperies, window shades and doors. The sender's comments may have been something of an exaggeration at that time, but are now more apt. C. 1905 [mvm]

CIRCUIT AVENUE: The well-known chronicler of Vineyard life and history, Henry Beetle Hough, once wrote: "the verandas and balconies were for sitting and watching the summer parade of vacationers. The avenue itself was more for strolling and shopping than for what is now transportation ... if some millionaire of the time ... could have assured the preservation of the old fantasy town, close kindred to the Camp Ground itself, what a living museum the island would possess today!" C. 1890 [mvm]

ISLAND DOCTOR: This is an early image of Circuit Avenue in Oak Bluffs looking south. The current view shows how little of that early streetscape remains and the change automobiles bring to perceiving it. The only building remaining is the Arcade, in the distance, just to the left of the rightmost column. The foreground sign is for Dr. W. Leach. A graduate of Harvard Medical School in 1856, he was this town's first year-round physician and served the community for forty years. Note the "Cottage City" signage. This was the town's baptismal name and it was not officially Oak Bluffs until 1907. C. 1890 [*mvm*]

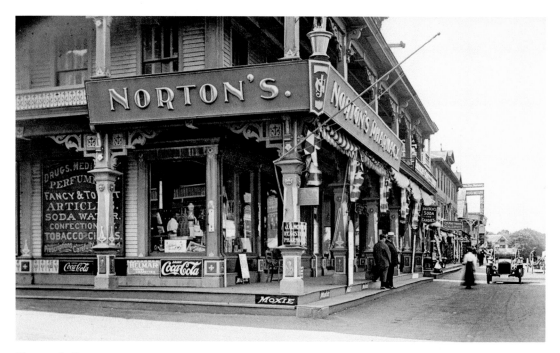

NORTON'S PHARMACY: Shown here is the pharmacy that once occupied one corner of the ground floor of the four storey Metropolitan Hotel built in the Second Empire style. This building demonstrated that architecture's function is not purely functional and practical. It is also symbolic. This too was destroyed by fire and replaced in 1946 by a one-storey collection of commercial properties and post office. The architectural style of what has replaced it is indeterminate. C. 1890 [*mvm*]

THE PAWNEE HOUSE: The Pawnee House opened in 1872 and immediately became one of the more popular accommodations on the island. "On Sunday afternoons, the Oak Bluffs Band would play from the balcony over the porch on the front. The rocking chairs all along the street level porch would be filled with people, sitting and rocking to the time of the music," remarked one early visitor. The elegance of its Empire Style was eviscerated when the top two floors were removed in 1953-54. The front arcade and ground floor of the original building are all that remain. C. 1890 [mvm]

THE OLD BOSTON HOUSE: This building is significant in that it is an example of the original architecture from the late 1800s that remains essentially intact. Several commercial ventures occupied it, including a popular Japanese goods shop (until the advent of WWII) and, later, Jimmy's Chicken by the Sea. It was vacant in the late 1970s when it became Linda Jean's, still open after nearly forty years. C. 1900 [mvm]

THE ARCADE: This is the oldest building on Circuit Avenue and a survivor from Oak Bluffs' Golden Age. Designed by Simon Freeman Pratt (Union Chapel), this building possesses integrity of design, craftsmanship, setting and association with the establishment and development of Oak Bluffs. It is an excellent example of Victorian Gothic architecture, preserving all the major elements of its original design, including the tiered porch with ornately carved balustrades. It also serves as a gateway to the Camp Ground, emphasizing the physical separation of the Camp Ground and Cottage City. C. 1890 [*mvm*]

DARLINGS: The advertising slogan, "For Twenty Years the Best," went unchanged for over sixty years. This was a popular stop on Circuit Avenue and an island landmark since Carroll J. Darling opened it in 1900. Flavored popcorn bars rivaled buttery white popcorn as an indulgence, but perhaps the most popular item was saltwater taffy. The taffy machine located in the front window always drew a small crowd as it stretched horse-collar sized lumps of the gelatinous material. Shown here is the machine in operation in 1975. It closed in 1981, to be replaced by part of the Murdick's Fudge chain. [*author*]

DINER NO MORE: William J. Ripley capitalized on the diner craze in America and went through three buildings before ending up with the 45-by-15-foot Nonpareil Diner on Lake Avenue across the street from The Tivoli. Shown here in the vintage photo are seven staff members behind the counter. Later, it became the popular Captain's Table and then an Asian restaurant. The diner building survives, but now houses a bicycle shop. Shown here is the new line-up, left to right: Willson, George and "J.B." C. 1935 [mvm]

SUNSET LAKE: This early view is of the skyline of Oak Bluffs looking east across Sunset Lake at the western edge of the Camp Ground. From left to right is the tower of the Sea View Hotel, the Baptist Temple, Trinity Methodist Church, The Tabernacle and Union Chapel. The footbridge, Sea View and temple are gone. But the rest remain, albeit now somewhat hidden by trees that here, as elsewhere, alter the view. C. 1880 [*mvm*]

HARBOR VIEW: This view looks across Oak Bluffs Harbor with the Sea View Hotel in the distance, placing this picture before 1882. The children stand at the beginning of the plank walk to the Highlands (compare it with the image following). The girls are wearing aprons over their frocks to minimize soiling and prolong their use. This view of Oak Bluffs Harbor was once considered the view over Jordan. At this time off-island Methodists arrived at the purpose-built dock in the Highlands and had to "cross over Jordan" to reach the sanctity of the Camp Ground. C. 1880 [mvm]

LOST PROMENADE: The top photo looks along what was once the public plank walk that bordered the west end of what is now Oak Bluffs Harbor. Just to the left of the sign "Promenade House," a popular guest house for the growing Black American community on the island can be made out. At the far end of the promenade the Highland House can be seen, also a popular resort for Black Americans in the Highlands section of Oak Bluffs. These establishments, and the promenade, are no longer. C. 1890 [mvm]

LAKE AVENUE: Looking east along Lake Avenue. The skating rink can be seen in the distance, placing this photo before 1882. The small row of cottages that today exist on the south side of Lake Avenue are above street level. Those shown in the top photo here are not, suggesting they were further along in an area where they were level with the street and no longer exist. What appears to be two buildings at the extreme left are actually one that still exists. Today, it houses an ice cream parlor. C. 1880 [*mvm*].

TRAFFIC LIGHT: At one time, there was "The Blinker," the island's only traffic light at the intersection of Old County Road with Barnes Road. The installation of a roundabout removed that light, leaving the island entirely free of traffic lights. But there once was one before that. In the top photo in front of the sedan at the right, a traffic light can be seen. The Strand Theatre is at the left, the ferry terminal straight ahead and the two towered Tivoli and Flying Horses at the right. C. 1935 [mvm]

THE TIVOLI: Opening in 1907, it had a rather slow start, but in ten years the Tivoli Ballroom had become the entertainment center of the island. By the 1930s, some of the best-known orchestras of the Big Band era played there. The second-floor ballroom had doors that opened onto a veranda and allowed the sound of the music to drift down into the street, while the evening breeze from the sound wafted in. The ground floor had a series of shops, a shooting gallery and a restaurant. It was torn down in 1964 and replaced by the Oak Bluffs Town Hall. C. 1915 [mvm]

ROLLER SKATING RINK: Built in 1879, it was a center of entertainment in Cottage City and the largest building on the island. The exterior style mimicked the armories found in mainland cities, but the interior had a smooth wooden floor and seating for over a thousand. Live music accompanied couples as they glided with views of the sea when the sliding walls were rolled back. The owner, Frank Winslow, designed the "Vineyard model" roller skate, sold worldwide. The rink was damaged by fire only three years later. Its original location would have been to the rear of the bank building shown. Shute. C. 1880 [*mvm*]

OCEAN PARK: When Cottage City was designed, its chief developer insisted on more open space, especially in the area where arriving ferry passengers were to disembark. The result was Ocean Park. This configuration and boundary of this space has changed little since its layout in 1866. Besides its nature as a welcoming threshold, it also performed as the common front lawn for the display of larger and more impressive cottages, whose design was inspired by those in the Camp Ground. In the top image, the roof of Pratt's Union Chapel can clearly be seen. C. 1880 [*mvm*]

OCEAN AVENUE
COTTAGE: Here, as
seen elsewhere, having
a photo of your cottage
taken was a significant
event and you dressed
and posed as if to add
to the adorning detail
of the cottage itself.
This building once
had finials, a ridge
line filigree, pointed
windows, and decorated
bargeboards that
proclaimed itself it to be
a "Cottage City cottage."
It has since been altered
beyond all recognition.
C. 1880 [mvm]

RIDAY'S COTTAGE: J. F. Riday's cottage (presumably Mr. Riday is shown lounging in front) on Ocean Ave is simple, yet with many of the features typical of the cottages that lined Ocean Avenue. The plank frame construction suggests that it was not, as many of the other cottages, winterized. Modern alterations seem to have taken the original design intent in a different direction. Edward L. Luce. 1880 [*mvm*]

49

LANDERS COTTAGE: This landmark cottage, also on Ocean Avenue, was distinctive even for Oak Bluffs, with an octagonal cupola that has been removed, as have many other tower-like features on other cottages. The exceptionally detailed cuts or carvings of animals on the projecting gable have been well preserved, but similar detail along the ground-floor railings, now hidden by shrubbery, has been altered. C. 1900 [mvm]

OCEAN AVENUE: The motivation for the creation of Ocean Park may have been more for profit than aesthetics, but it was design brilliance all the same. Its open form not only gave visitors a sense of welcome, but it also both edged the park and was a presentation of the architecture Cottage City had become famous for. Shown here are the cottages along the northern end. Here, as elsewhere, the automobile diminishes the experience of that same perspective. C. 1880 [mvm]

PEQUOT AVE HOUSE: With its scrolled verge boards, steeply pitched roof, and wrap-around porch, this house on Pequot Avenue reflected the design intent of the master plan for this new town. The most visible and most common element shared elsewhere is the porch, an open invitation for interchange between strangers. Is idyll time better enjoyed anywhere else? C. 1880 [*mvm*]

WINIFRED HOUSE: A strong example of vernacular vineyard architecture in the Carpenter Gothic style with hooded dormers, steep rooflines and extravagant scrollwork. One of the first black owned establishments on the island, it appears on an 1887 Sanborn map. It lasted approximately 100 years on Pequot Ave in Oak Bluffs. The porch was not only a design feature, it was a social device. The two residential buildings that replaced it have suburban-style setbacks, thus ending chance greetings between people on the porch and passersby. C. 1912 [*J. N. Chamberlain*]

A PRATT HOUSE: Samuel Freeman Pratt was perhaps the most popular architect during Oak Bluffs boom building period in the 1870s. This cottage built by the Howland family typified the originality of his rooflines, as well as a whole panoply of secular Gothic elements. Curiously, he only built on the island, thus adding to its already architectural distinctiveness. Pratt's characteristic treatment of a large roof perched atop a "smaller" house has been altered, along with the much of the articulated verge board. C. 1870 [*mvm*]

NARAGANSETT AVENUE: The cottages along this street give testimony to the fact that the architects and builders in Cottage City, seeking to outdo their Camp Ground neighbors, emulated, copied, transmuted and reflected the elaborate architecture that had already gained a foothold in that community. Narragansett Avenue, as well nearby Pequot and Samoset Avenues, curve in sympathy with the defining arc of Ocean Avenue, thus avoiding a grid-like design plan. C. 1890 [*source unknown*]

UNION CHAPEL: One of Pratt's outstanding works is the octagonal Union Chapel. Built in 1870, it exemplifies Pratt's tendency for strong geometry. Its purpose, as an interdenominational church, was to serve summer visitors reluctant to mix with a more rigid Camp Ground culture. Only five days after the fire that destroyed Vineyard Haven, it advertised "Grand Music and Dramatic Entertainment in Aid of the Vineyard Haven Relief Fund." The modern view shows not only a much-altered structure, but one now hidden by trees whose original purpose may have been otherwise. C. 1870 [mvm]

THE CENTRAL HOUSE: Later known as the Beatrice House, it survived until about 1930. It was a last stop before leaving the Camp Ground and passing through the Arcade onto Circuit Avenue. As Cottage City grew, the Wesleyan Methodist community added to the amenities within its own confines to keep summertime members from straying over into temptation on Circuit Avenue. The construction of Central House was one result of this. When built, it was the largest building within the Camp Ground community. C. 1890 [*mvm*]

THE FIRST WOODEN
COTTAGE: Technically, this
may have been a wooden hut
built in the mid-1850s, but
the Mason- Lawton cottage
shown initiated the style that
introduced the Camp Ground
cottage motif: oversized
double doors, an overhead
balcony and small second
story doors. Its significance
lies in the fact that it became
the prototype for design and
construction leading to the
unified appearance of the
Camp Ground cottages that
later followed. The modern
perspective is, unfortunately,
marred by a telephone pole.
C. 1859 [mvm]

PRESIDENT'S GRANT'S VISIT: Whatever his reason, political or otherwise, Grant's three-day visit in 1874 served to elevate the status of Martha's Vineyard as a summer destination. Here he is shown at what was Bishop Haven's cottage on Clinton Avenue in the Camp Ground with the First Lady and others. He later dined at the Central House (page 57) and watched fireworks in his honor in Ocean Park. C. 1874 [*mvm*]

THE SCROLL SAW: The details shown on Camp Ground cottage verge boards are the result of the heavily adopted scroll saw. This was a vertical blade driven by a foot-powered treadle. Its key innovation was the pierce cut, an internal cut made without cutting through the sides or edges. Shown here on Hunters Cottage is a rabbit being chased, over the decades, by a dog. Cottages in the Camp Ground and along Ocean Ave (e.g. Tucker Cottage) are replete with such animal carvings. C. 1890 [*mvm*]

THE TABERNACLE EXTERIOR: This unusual structure holds a place in both the annals of architecture as well local history. Built by the firm of Dwight and Hoyt of Boston for a little over $7,000, it was half the price of a wooden structure. Completed in 1879, it fulfilled the needs for stability, warmth in winter and coolness in summer. There is little documentation as to the design intent of its architect, and less easy to catalogue as a building type except to say that it is distinctly American. The modern view, taken from the same vantage point as the top photo, is now blocked by trees. C. 1890 [mvm]

THE TABERNACLE INTERIOR: The innovative design of this remarkable structure is best appreciated from the inside where the structural web of wrought-iron supports is left visible to allow the viewer to appreciate its ingenuity. There are only four interior columns that give the three-tiered roofs a sense of lightness, a floating that echoes that of the fan vaulting of those Gothic cathedrals that influenced, in spirit at least, the architecture of the Camp Ground cottages around it. It is a magical place within a place. C. 1890 [mvm]

SANITARY LAUNDRY: The Camp Ground sought to remain a self-contained community as the commercial venture built to attract the summer visitor expanded outside it. Separate agendas led to their not designing in concert. As Cottage City began to be realized, a seven-foot wall was built around the Camp Ground to insulate it from secular influences. Shown here was the community laundry built on the western edge of the Camp Ground site. No longer a laundry, the building now contains apartments. C. 1890 [mvm]

THE MARTHA'S VINEYARD SUMMER INSTITUTE: The institute was located near what is now the East Chop Beach Club (an area once more frequently referred to as The Highlands). It had the distinction of being the first summer school for teachers in the country. The courses offered included botany, archeology elocution, rhetoric and English literature. Mainland colleges later copied this model, but also offered regular credit towards a degree, something the institute did not. It could not compete and closed its doors in 1907. C. 1898 [*The Rotograph Co.*]

VINEYARD HAVEN: The 1883 fire "cut the heart out of a beautiful village." Not much photographic preservation of it remains, such as this this rural-like view of the beginning of Main Street. It is probable that few of the structures shown here would have survived even without the fire, except perhaps for the church. The basic layout remains, but the architecture, especially that of the new Mansion House on the right, shows how much has been altered. C. 1880 [*mvm*]

MAIN STREET: This early view of Main Street shows a grocery at left and the structure with the gable projection at the center of the image was the site of its second library. The prior building, destroyed by the 1883 fire, housed the first library on the island. This replacement bears traces of the Queen Anne style, unusual for a high street on the island. The difference between the architectural character of this street and that of Oak Bluffs and Edgartown is noteworthy. C. 1900 [mvm]

THE CAPOWACK CINEMA: Opened in 1913 during the silent film era, it survives, in part, because there will not be a suburban multiplex alternative. The architectural style, remarkably unremarkable, contributes to its character. After a two-year hiatus, it reopened in 2015 after an interior renovation and now has a modest 220-seat capacity. Note that in the top image the sign reads "Capowack" while it reads "Capawock" in the bottom, either one likely a phonetic of the Wampanoag word for "place of refuge. C. 1910 [*mvm*]

THE OLD LIVERY STABLE: This was once the Norton Family Livery Stable that here highlights its island location with nauticalia over the bays. The sign at right advertises a play, "The Late Christopher Bean," that dates the photo at around 1933. This site became the home of a trendy housewares shop for many years and then a bookstore. It today stands empty. C. 1933 [*mvm*]

THE LUCE STORE: Within weeks after the great August 1883 fire, the *Vineyard Gazette* reported that Mr. Stephen C. Luce of Tisbury had "purchased the lot at the corner of Main and Franklin (now Church) Streets for the site of a store which is to be built for his grocery business." The horse and cart in the front were for deliveries. Immediately to the left is the telephone exchange. The grocery store is no longer there, but the building remains to meet the needs of summer visitors. C. 1900 [*mvm*]

THE STONE BUILDING: This building, designed in 1905, for many years housed a bank. It is a rare example of the Romanesque style on Martha's Vineyard with elements of the Bungalow style intermixed. An overhanging roof of terra-cotta tile extends beyond the façade of locally found fieldstone. An arched entrance and deep-set windows relieve the massiveness of the structure. The terra-cotta tiles have been, controversially, removed and replaced with red tinted shingles. The building now stands empty. C. 1910 [*mvm*]

OLD DAR BUILDING: Built in 1828, it is the island's oldest surviving one-room schoolhouse. It survived the 1883 fire that destroyed the rest of Main Street. In 1775, the captain of the British warship *Unicorn* announced that the Liberty Tree, a town landmark, was to be cut down for use in repairing a mast. Three young girls prevented this by destroying it with gunpowder. A plaque with their names on the flagpole shown commemorates this event. The building is now used for educational workshops and social gatherings. C. 1890 [*mvm*]

TISBURY TOWN HALL: Built in 1844 as a Congregational Church, the building has gone through many uses. In 1884, it was purchased by the Vineyard Literary Association, hence the later name of Association Hall. The town purchased it in 1920 and still uses it for town offices. Another major alteration came when Katherine Cornell and fellow trustees converted the second floor to a theater space. The front façade can be considered "New England Classical" and the pediment displays a richly embellished sculpture based on the town seal. C. 1890 [mvm]

St Augustine's Church: This early photograph shows three young girls walking towards St. Augustine's Roman Catholic Church in Vineyard Haven. Its location, at the intersection of Pine and Spring Streets, illustrates how rural Vineyard Haven was in the 1930s just a few blocks from Main Street. The building currently houses the office of the superintendent of schools. C. 1933 [*hne*]

LAGOON POND: Lagoon Pond in Tisbury and Oak Bluffs is a naturally deep tidal lagoon, about two miles long and over one-third mile wide. It was not possible to produce the modern photograph from the same historic viewpoint as that portion of Lagoon Pond shown in the top image has been filled in (sometime after 1913 when it is shown on Eldridge's map). The large building at left on the hill is the former marine hospital and the Martha's Vineyard Museum today. C. 1900 [*mvm*]

TASHMOO SPRINGS PUMPING STATION: The facility was constructed to meet the need for a safe water supply and to provide economic, recreational and physical growth for Vineyard Haven. Built in 1887 on Lake Tashmoo, this expression of Late Victorian, Colonial Revival architecture is significant as the earliest known water works on the island. It closed in 1971, but has been restored and used for private functions. The viewpoint of the original photo is now on private property. C. 1890 [*mvm*]

THE EARLY AIRPORT: The Martha's Vineyard airport had its beginnings in September 1942 with the construction of a small airfield built to train Navy pilots. The land, over 600 acres, had been sold to the government for one dollar. Shown here are the two-story wooden barracks where the enlisted men stayed. The transient aircrews came for six weeks of intensive training and had little time to enjoy the island, but some did return to make it their home. Airport parking now occupies the spot where these barracks once stood. C. 1943 [*mvm*]

THE BUNKER: During the Second World War, coastal German U-Boat activity was a major concern. Shown here in the top photo are the remains of a bunker built on South Beach to not only watch for surfaced submarines, but also for the saboteurs and spies rumored to have slipped ashore. By the 1970s, when the top photo was taken, the bunker only served as rendezvous point for beachgoers. The location of the bottom photo is only an approximation as the bunker is now beneath the surface of the encroaching sea. [*author*]

LAMBERT'S COVE METHODIST CHURCH: Its construction in 1846 was charged by a committee to "agree with a carpenter ... to build the said meeting house as cheap as they can." The result has lasted 175 years and was the first Methodist church on the island. In 2010, a dwindling congregation and maintenance costs forced its closure and its bell no longer announces Sunday services, weddings or funerals. It is now a "sumptuous summer residential getaway" that provides visitors a "true island experience with the amenities of a boutique hotel." C. 1890 [*mvm*]

AN ISLAND SURVIVOR: Located on State Road as you head up-Island, this building once housed the Middleton Post Office, so named before the establishment of the town of West Tisbury. Its clean lines, proportions and corner pilasters are elements of the Greek Revival style popular on the island at the time. The sign at right reads "Local Long Distance Telephone." It became the popular Red Cat Bookstore in 1959 until its closure in the 1980s. It is now a clothing boutique. Edward Lee Luce. C. 1890 [mvm]

SATINET MILL: Located on Old Mill Pond at the intersection of Edgartown Road and State Road, its construction brought the Industrial Revolution to Martha's Vineyard. Prior to this, woven cloth was produced in private homes. The cloth it wove from local island wool was Satinet. Heavy, warm and flexible it was popular with whalemen. It sold in three colors: "black and light or dark brown for $1.25 per yard," as an early advertisement proclaimed. C. 1875 [*mvm*]

ALLEY'S GENERAL STORE: More than a general store, it is also a place to reminisce. This building is an island icon through its history and location. It is both the oldest retail business on Martha's Vineyard and has a way of punctuating the journey down-or up-Island. Opened since 1858, it provides staples for local fishermen and farmers as well as the casual traveler who may wish to purchase classic candy or flower seeds with their coffee. Representing both longevity and stability, it is a premier gathering spot for locals and visitors alike. C. 1890 [*mvm*]

THE GRANGE HALL: Built in 1859, this is the center, figuratively and literally, of island agriculture and commerce. It is also an enduring landmark whose annual cattle show and fair was once described as "more than a frolicsome, frivolous and ephemeral affair ... how happy people were in meeting one another! Maids and matrons, youths and veterans, old-timers, and newcomers, sea captains, physicians, politicians, lawyers, clergymen, agriculturalists, rollicking boys and girls, pupils, sweet little tots, proud parents, this is a composite photograph of those who come from every direction of the Island." C. 1890 [mvm]

WEST TISBURY CENTER: The center of West Tisbury has changed little over the years, except for the tree growth that makes it less easy to appreciate the architecture. Shown in the top photo are the West Congregational Church and the once famous Dukes County Academy that later became West Tisbury's elementary school. The church survived many alterations and locations as well as the inroads of evangelical Protestantism over the years and remains a mainstay of the local community. C. 1890 [mvm]

WEST TISBURY TOWN HALL: Formerly the Dukes County Academy and the later an elementary school, it now serves and the West Tisbury Town Hall. It may appear that the school once kept chickens, but the coop in the foreground is likely part of the annual Grange Fair show. The Grange Hall is directly to the rear of the viewer and the fence that separates its property from that of the school can be seen in the top photograph. C. 1890 [mvm]

THE OLD LIBRARY BUILDING: Running perpendicular to State Road between the West Congregational Church and former elementary school is Music Street. This was allegedly so named because of the number of pianos in the homes there, heard played through open windows. The library began in the Dukes County Academy, but was later moved to this building on Music Street in 1893. It served as the home of the library for 100 years and is now administered by the Island Preservation Trust. C. 1890 [*mvm*]

WEST TISBURY ELEMENTARY SCHOOL: This building first housed the Dukes County Academy that taught whalemen mathematics, navigation and astronomy. It then became the local elementary school. An early account: "At recess the boys played ball in the playground. The older girls walked arm-in-arm two by two ... the younger ones played London Bridge is Falling Down, singing out of key. At noon we sat on the fence between the school and the Agricultural Hall to eat our lunches, then balanced on the fence like circus performers. The bell rang, and we reluctantly went inside." The building now houses the West Tisbury Town Hall. C. 1910 [*mvm*]

MENEMSHA VIEW: The island's only fishing village, the cancellation stamp at its first post office read "Creekville, Mass." The settlement there did indeed line the creek that wended its way into the Atlantic. After it was dredged, widened and made more navigable, the name change was made in 1913. Menemsha, or "still waters," grew, but the devastating 1938 hurricane swept away most of the low-lying buildings. Shown here in the above image is its pre-hurricane appearance and the bottom image was made from Dutcher Dock, part of the subsequent rebuild. C. 1935 [mvm]

DUTCHER DOCK: The Great New England Hurricane of 1938 swept the fishing village of Menemsha into Vineyard Sound. Rodney Dutcher, a Vineyard native, witnessed it and began the effort to secure the federal assistance to rebuild this devasted community. Shown in the top image is the dedication ceremony of the new wharf facilities in 1941. He died of heart failure before having a chance to see the fruits of his efforts, but a grateful and restored Menemsha remembers. [*mvm*]

SWORDFISH FLEET: Shown here in the top photo is Menemsha swordfish fleet at anchor. The 1938 hurricane gave this industry a crippling blow. It slowly rebounded, but later overfishing plus the decline and location of the swordfish population forced the close of commercial sword fishing here. It has since been reinstated to allow for both recreational and commercial fishing, but it has not returned to the pre-hurricane heyday when even mainland sword fishermen would use Menemsha basin as their base. C. 1935 [mvm]

CHILMARK TOWN HALL: Built in 1897, it is relatively modern, as things go on Martha's Vineyard. Until 1956 it also served as the Chilmark Community Center, now located nearby. The Greek Revival architectural exterior remains, a popular style designated for public use. It is the only building of this style in Chilmark but is similar to other public buildings on the island. C. 1890 [*mvm*]

CHILMARK SCHOOL: Also referred to as the Menemsha school it was once, together with the town's post office, library, town hall, community center and fire station, an integral part of the village of Chilmark's life and history. It remained a school until the 1980s. Despite the obvious change of use, the density and character of Chilmark town center has changed little over the years. C. 1890 [*mvm*]

BEETLEBUNG CORNER: At the intersection of South Road, Middle Road and Menemsha Cross Rd, this corner is the Chilmark's town center. It is so labeled, because it is one of two locations where a species of *Nyssa sylvatica* unique to this island grows. The center, once consisting of a blacksmith shop and general store, has changed little over the years. A similar intersection on the mainland might well have been developed with fast food franchises spreading in all directions. C. 1940 [*mvm*]

A VIEW IN CHILMARK: The top image looks east just before the spot where State Road crosses Nashaquitsa Pond (slightly in view at left) and Stonewall Pond on the right, out of view. Chilmark, at the time of this photograph, was known for its long views, worth standing on top of a granite column for. The bottom image shows how here, as elsewhere, reforestation has transformed perception of this landscape. C. 1900 [*mvm*]

GAY HEAD LIGHT: Gay Head Light, located at the southwestern most point of land on the island that continues to be a mixture of a touristic, nautical and Native-American landscape. The Not-O-Way Inn and other outbuilding shown no longer remain. The light once used a Fresnel lens with 1,008 prisms, now on display at the Martha's Vineyard Museum. This site also contains Aquinnah's only commercial activities, local family owned and operated souvenir shops, food services for tour buses and cars that park on the large asphalt lot below the lighthouse on Wampanoag Tribal common lands. C. 1935 [*American Art Post Card Co.*]

Acknowledgements

First, I thank Bow Van Riper of the Martha's Vineyard Museum for his hospitality and the unflagging support that has made this book possible. Christine Seidel of the Martha's Vineyard Commission provided the necessary cartographic tools, and Hilary Wall of the *Vineyard Gazette* the background story to much of what is contained within. Durwood Vanderhoop also kindly assisted with Wampanoag translation.

In traveling around the island to secure the contemporary photographs, I was frequently assisted by island residents themselves. I thank Donna Leon, Robert Gatchell, Doug Thomson, Tim Donahue, Aesha Mumin, Sarah Keena, Bill Roman, Thomas Fisher, Kathryn Allen, Dick Miller, Kevin L. Searle, John and Diane Maguire, Harold Chapdelaine, Robin Wilson, Nancy Crossley Black and Mark Wallace. Their warm receptions and eagerness to help made this project much less taxing and much more memorable.

Photo and Map Credits

hne	Historic New England
loc	Library of Congress
macris	Courtesy Office of the Secretary of the Commonwealth William F. Galvin, Massachusetts Historical Commission
mvc	Maps compiled by Chris Seidel of the Martha's Vineyard Commission, 2019
mvm	Martha's Vineyard Museum

FRONT COVER
Top: mvm
Bottom: the author

BACK COVER
Top: detail from image page 17
Bottom: the author

SUGGESTED READING

A. Bowdoin Van Riper, *Edgartown*, Arcadia Pub., 2018

Allen, Joseph C., *Tails and Trails of Martha's Vineyard*, Little, Brown and Co., 1938

Banks, Charles E. & Dean, George H., *The History of Martha's Vineyard Dukes County Vol II Town Annals*, George H. Dean, 1911

Dresser, Thos., *Hidden History of Martha's Vineyard*, The History Press, 2017

Foster, David R., *A Meeting of Land and Sea*, Yale University Press, 2017

Gookin, Warner Foote, B.D, *Capawack alias Martha's Vineyard*, Dukes County Historical Society, Edgartown MA, 1947

Hine, C. G., *The Story of Martha's Vineyard*, Hine Bros., 1908

Hough, Henry Beetle, *Martha's Vineyard; Summer Resort 1835-1935*, Tuttle Pub., 1936

Hough, Henry Beetle, *Singing in the Morning and Other Essays About Martha's Vineyard*, Simon and Schuster, 1951

Huntington, Gale, *An Introduction to Martha's Vineyard*, Martha's Vineyard Print Co., 1969

Martha's Vineyard Commission, *Island Plan; Charting the Future of the Vineyard*, MV Commission, 2010

No author given, *Fifty Glimpses of Martha's Vineyard*, Rand McNally, 1900

Simon, Anne W., *No Island Is an Island, The Ordeal of Martha's Vineyard*, Doubleday and Company, 1973

Railton, Arthur R., *The History of Martha's Vineyard*, Commonwealth Editions, 2006

Safford, Nancy, *Time's Island, Portraits of the Vineyard*, MIT Press, 1973

Simon, Peter, *On the Vineyard*, Anchor Books, 1980

Smith, Wayne and Stacy, Bonnie, *Island Stories*, Martha's Vineyard Museum, 2015

Weiss, Ellen, *City in the Woods*, Oxford University Press, 1987